Writing a Research Paper

Quick and Easy Guide

Anna Georgantonis Keah

Illustrations by Sharolyn Swan

Footsteps Publications

The Educational Publisher
Columbus, Ohio

**Footsteps Publications
Austin, Texas**

www.EduPublisher.com

© 2009, 2011, 2012 The Educational Publisher
All rights reserved. Published 2009. Second Edition 2011,
Third Edition 2012

No part of this book may be used or
reproduced in any manner whatsoever
without the written permission of the Publisher.

ISBN 978-1-62249-019-6

Printed in the United States of America

*To the memory of Sharolyn Swan
whose kind guidance and unfailing support
made this publication possible ...
May her spirit rest in peace.*

Table of Contents

Step 1	Choosing a Topic and Title	7
Step 2	Preliminary Search	10
Step 3	Mind Map and Thesis Statement	12
Step 4	Headings	16
Step 5	Finding Source Materials	18
Step 6	Taking Notes	22
Step 7	Outline	24
Step 8	Rough Draft	29
Step 9	Editing	33
Step 10	Final Copy	38

MLA Format Guidelines.........................40

Research Styles................................42

Sample MLA Research Paper..................43

APA Format Guidelines........................64

Sample APA Research Paper..................67

Research Topic Ideas...........................91

Foreword

In preparing the third edition of this booklet, it became obvious that adding APA style was essential. Most professors require either MLA or APA style, and so a sample APA paper was added in addition to a list of APA requirements. This opens the booklet up to a much wider audience and will certainly prove valuable to many more students and teachers.

It is my great hope that students and teachers alike will make this small booklet a part of their academic lives and enjoy using it as much as I enjoyed creating it.

Introduction

After years of teaching thousands of students and grading approximately that many research papers, a professor starts to get an idea about how to teach the research process. I finally came to the realization that if I taught well, my students wrote some amazingly high quality papers, and grading became much easier. The result is this simple, ten-step approach to writing a well-organized, quality research paper.

These ten easy steps will guide your research effort from choosing a topic to writing the rough draft to the final quality product. I wrote a research paper, one in MLA style and one in APA style, specifically for this booklet as an example of this technique and have used the mind map and outline from the booklet to demonstrate my research method. In this way, you will be able to feel the research experience in action from beginning to end. Most of the examples in the steps refer to MLA style; however, I have included a section on APA style as well.

From the mind map to the outline to the actual paper, you can follow the step-by-step progression of writing an excellent research paper, and once you write one successful, quality research paper, the rest are a piece of cake!

ONE

Step 1 Choosing a Topic and Title

Always select a topic which truly interests you. Your enthusiasm will carry you through to the end. Remember to be specific: find a small plot and dig deep.

First of all, let me explain the most important aspect of this approach. *YOU* are the *author* of this paper. You are the one driving the boat. You are the one interpreting the information you find, and you are passing it on to others so that they can share in your discovery. It is *your* project.

For that reason, you need to choose a topic that both challenges and interests you, one that you would read about if you had a sunny day at the beach and nowhere to go. Sometimes you have a choice about choosing a topic and sometimes you don't according to the class requirements. If you have the opportunity to choose your topic, look at the possible topics at the back of this booklet for some creative ideas on areas to research! After choosing your topic, create a title in the form of a question.

Hint: Look in your own collection of books to get ideas about your topic.

How *I* Did It...

Choosing a topic was a difficult process for me. Before I decided on a topic for the sample research paper in this booklet, I went through LOTS of topics. I asked myself many questions. What will students be interested in reading? What will really keep them involved? I was getting nowhere. Every time I came up with something I thought would "sell" students, I lost interest in the topic.

Finally, I backed off and decided to look at what would interest ME! After all, that was my advice to you, my students! At the time, I had been newly diagnosed with a stress-related illness. I was quite ill, barely getting up and down steps, fatigued and in pain. All of a sudden, I had a topic in which I had a vested interest: I wanted to get better. Now it became MY topic, and as a result of my research, guess what? I am remarkably better, not running up and down steps but so much improved! I am so glad I chose that topic. I learned more about my health and myself than a doctor could ever have taught me.

You HAVE to choose a topic that is of value to you at some level—academic, personal, emotional, physical, intellectual, spiritual—or all of the above. You have to have some vested interest in pursuing this research.

This driving fascination will not only carry you through to the end but also will allow you to create something of true worth and value, something more than just the fulfillment of a class requirement. "Research" means we are setting out to explore something of interest about which we want to increase our knowledge. Do some soul searching before choosing your topic.

TWO

Step 2 Preliminary Search

After choosing your topic, do a preliminary search on the internet and in the library to make sure there is enough material on your subject and also to make sure that your topic is not too broad. Use keywords to guide your search.

The purpose of the preliminary search is to make sure your topic is not too broad or too narrow. Remember to be very open to what you find. Use many different keywords to do your search, changing them often to open up new possibilities. Print a few articles and review them briefly to see if you want to read further. Save them for future use in your paper. At this point, your topic can change since you are still exploring the subject.

You will find yourself drawn to books and articles which reflect your genuine areas of interest, and the research trail will take you in the direction YOU choose to go!

By the way, librarians love it when you ask for help. They can show you databases and materials very specific to your subject—resources you might never have found if you had not asked for help. Go ahead...Make a librarian's day!

> **Hint: Go to the library to get great help with finding information.**

How *I* Did It...

The preliminary search started out pretty easy for me. After all, I am an English teacher, so the first thing I did was to look at my own collection of books to see if I could use any of them in my research. Unfortunately, I have very few health books, and I did not have any specific books on the subject of fibromyalgia since my diagnosis was relatively new. The books I do have on health, however, are very old and very basic, so I started out by reading about healthy living in general. As it turns out, my research revealed that getting better with this diagnosis means a lifestyle change as is true with so much illness. After my research, at least part of my plan has been to go back to the basics I read about in my health books of the past, the ones I reviewed during my preliminary search.

This does not mean YOU will not find really good sources in your own collection of books about your subject. You DO have a "library" whether you know it or not. Look there first. Chances are if you are excited about your topic, it is something you have explored.

Next, I did an internet search on stress-related disease which included causes, types, symptoms, traditional treatments, alternative cures, anything to help me better understand why I developed this illness and what was going to make me better.

When you do your preliminary search, really think about different combinations of keywords to check out your topic. The idea is to review different articles about your subject. If you find an article that really intrigues you, go ahead and make a copy of it for future use, or you could just bookmark the website. The important thing is to start the process of finding sources of information. Be careful that you do not spend too much time with no results.

THREE

Step 3 Mind Map and Thesis Statement

Create a mind map in the form of a bubble chart as you brainstorm about what you know of the topic including information from your preliminary search for sources.

After your preliminary review, make a mind map which is a bubble chart of your knowledge on the subject. Write down everything that you can think of about your topic, insights you had before and after the preliminary review. As you think of one aspect, branch off into other aspects. The idea is to take a snapshot of what you currently know or want to explore about your topic. This is a spontaneous, freethinking exercise. It does not have to be organized and formal. Get your creative juices flowing!

In this brainstorming process, you will collect more information than you will need, and you will use it as a means of narrowing down and better understanding various aspects of your topic that interest you. Construct a thesis statement, one sentence that summarizes the main point of your paper and include it on the first page of your paper.

Hint: The mind map becomes the springboard to your research project.

This is not a time to hold back. Write down everything that you can possibly think of that relates to your topic. You will be surprised at how much detail will come to mind once you get started. If you have chosen a good solid topic that thoroughly intrigues you, the mind map will flow easily. If you are struggling, perhaps this is the time to change your topic. The mind map really is a blueprint of your brain about your interest in and understanding of your chosen topic.

As you think about your topic, notice that major categories or areas of interest begin to develop. Write them down, and then branch off from these key areas of interest into more detail. The more detailed your mind map is, the easier it will be to write your outline later. You are not going to use everything on the mind map on your outline or even in your paper, but the brainstorming session will help you pinpoint what really interests you about the subject. You might only use half of the information on the mind map, but at least you will know why you picked the topic and where you want to go with it ultimately. You will be surprised at how much you already know about the subject and the many aspects that are yet to be explored. The mind map truly is the fertile ground from which your research paper will spring to life.

Hint: Imagine your mind is a blank page then fill it up with ideas, thoughts and reflections about your topic.

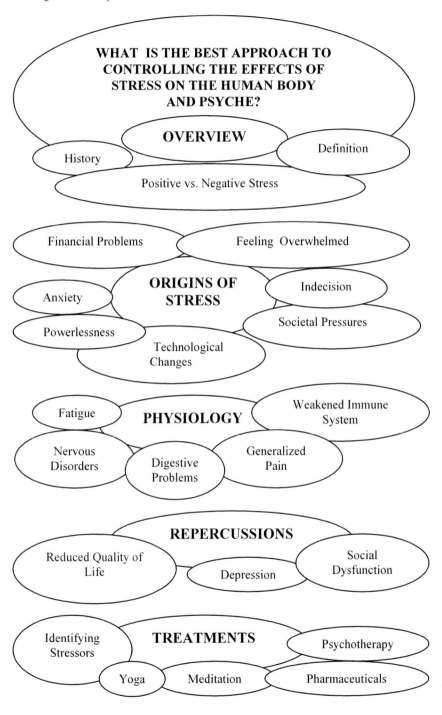

How *I* Did It...

My mind map was relatively easy since I had explored my topic from the personal perspective of my illness and had also spent some time on the internet doing my preliminary search. As I brainstormed, I remembered to include major areas of interest about my subject. I listed these major categories and started writing down everything I could think of related to my knowledge of stress. I really had not thought about it that much. At first, I included my knowledge about the illness from personal experience, then I started freethinking about what I had discovered on the internet. It is not that difficult to brainstorm about the many aspects of a topic if you have had some personal experience with it. I started to list my symptoms, both physical and emotional. I explored ways that this illness had changed my life. I tried to pinpoint potential causes. In short, I racked my brain on every aspect of my life since I had been diagnosed with fibromyalgia. After I reviewed a few articles, I was able to compare what I had read with what I was experiencing. I recorded all this information on my mind map which was soon a combination of what I knew and what I still needed to find out.

My mind map gave me a starting point on which to build my research. It gave me the impetus to go forward. It truly offered the motivation to move forward with my paper. I have, in the past, constructed even more than one mind map.

After the mind map, it is a good idea to construct a thesis statement, which is a summary statement describing your main point. The thesis statement should appear in the first paragraph of your paper. It can help keep you on track as far as the purpose of your research. My thesis statement is the last sentence in bold of the first paragraph of the sample papers at the back of this booklet. Review them for a good example of a strong thesis statement.

FOUR

Step 4 Headings

From the mind map, identify five to seven major headings for your research paper. This is called the classification pattern of writing.

Major headings will organize your research topic into manageable categories, and they will form the Roman numerals for your outline. In addition, the headings will be placed into the body of your paper so that not only is your paper easier to write, it is easier to read.

This pattern of writing is called "classifying" since you are taking bits of information and classifying them into major common areas. By creating these categories early on, you will have a guide to follow when sorting out all the data you discover.

I.   **Overview**
II.   **Origins of Stress**
III.   **Repercussions of Stress-Related Disease**
IV.   **Physiology of Stress**
V.   **Treatment of Stress-Related Disease**
VI.   **Findings**

Hint: Use your headings as the Roman numerals for your outline.

How *I* Did It...

I knew the **headings** for my paper would somehow evolve from the mind map, so I kept that in mind as I was brainstorming. I tried to think of major categories that interested me, problems I had actually encountered with my illness.

When I went back to review my mind map in search of headings, they just seemed to jump out at me. The headings I ended up choosing were clearly logical dividers for the many aspects of my topic: Overview, Origins, Repercussions, Physiology, Treatment and Findings.

I had really combed my mind to determine these headings and had given it much thought. For my first heading, I knew I wanted something introductory: Overview, Definition, History or Background. For my final heading, I wanted to prepare my audience for a definitive ending: Conclusions, Findings, Recommendations, Observations, or Deductions.

After deciding on my headings, my thoughts truly took a different turn. I could organize my research through these categories. By creating these subject areas, my review of sources could now become more organized. As I was drawn to facts and data that interested me, I was able to classify this information into the areas of my research.

After the headings fell into place, I even went back and added more to my mind map. There was something about listing the headings that seemed to make my research effort gel. I was able to categorize every piece of information I came across, then I could focus on organizing all that data within each category. Creating headings truly gave me a sense of organization and, ultimately, a well-organized research effort.

FIVE

Step 5 Finding Source Materials

Find 10-20 sources on your topic. You can find materials on the internet, in libraries, on databases, and even in your own collection of books. Remember that the internet *contains* many sources but is not considered a source in and of itself.

Seek out lots of articles and materials on your topic. The more information you read, including opposing views and perceptions different from your own, the better you will understand your topic and the more interesting your paper will be. You probably will not use all the materials you review. By the way, remember to staple articles as you print them in order to keep track of all that paper.

Academic sources include books; articles from periodicals, journals, magazines, and newspapers; pamphlets; TV documentaries; videos; personal and professional interviews and the list goes on and on. Be creative in looking for sources. The sky's the limit!

> **Hint: TV documentaries can be an interesting source of information for your paper.**

With so much information at our fingertips these days, there is an endless supply of sources of data. You want to really scrutinize everything you read. Just because it is in print doesn't necessarily mean it is a valid, documented source.

Usually, if you are reading something with a bibliography, the author has done his/her homework in researching the subject. Look over the source before you start reviewing it. Does it have an author and publication date? Is it an excerpt from a larger work?

Conducting an interview yourself is a very valuable way to obtain information. When interviewing someone in person, it is a good idea to tape the conversation WITH the permission of the person being interviewed. Often, you can email a professional, author or expert in the field with carefully constructed interview questions, and they will respond. So many of my students have done so and been surprised with the results. It's worth a try!

Hint: Before your interview, think up four or five interesting questions to ask the person you are interviewing. Be imaginative!

The internet can be a great way to find materials, but you really have to be careful about what you pull up. Websites can be credible sources, but you have to verify that to yourself. What are the credentials of the experts giving information?

Whenever possible, print articles so that you can take notes in the margins as you read them. Materials can be copied as long as your intention is to use them for strictly academic purposes and not for profit. If watching a TV documentary or video, take notes and make sure to write down the time, date and name of the program.

Your school library or the public library contains a wealth of information AND librarians to assist you in wading through it. Your school library will have subject-specific databases which contain articles by subject. Some examples are PsychLit, InfoTrac and others. These databases include only scholarly articles in the field, allowing you to search for reliable sources. Feel free to explore alternative sources, however, in search of the truth. The internet has given us access to all sorts of investigative sources that research topics thoroughly. "Mainstream media" is not always the most reliable and completely documented source. Explore other options in your pursuit of truth. Look into alternative news sources.

Hint: Make sure the websites you use are reliable sources.

How *I* Did It...

Finding source materials was a little difficult because my mobility was rather limited at the time, so I did much of my research on the internet. I did, however, manage to go to the public library and access some information. While surfing the net, I was very careful about what to use. Before I even reviewed an article, I checked it for reliability. If it did not have an author or if I could not verify the origin or credentials of the writer, I did not always use the article unless it was a reputable website. In this day and age, ANYONE can post information on the web, so I was very discerning about what I chose to research for my paper.

I collected MANY articles! As a matter of fact, I did not use a number of the articles I found. My goal was to set up a broad spectrum of data. I did a brief review, and if I thought there was a remote possibility I might use the article for my paper, I copied it. I always stapled my articles as soon as I printed them since I can sometimes be disorganized about paperwork!

I started looking out for articles in the local newspaper and TV documentaries that covered my topic. When you put out feelers like this, it is amazing what will come to you. The research project really became a part of my everyday coming and going. I was determined to find out all I could about stress-related disease. I talked to people to find out what others were doing to deal with this illness.

In the end, I found out that 80% of all illness is stress-related! Wow! Not just my little disease but *many* others were impacted by stress. I was now ready and equipped to get down to the bottom of the issue!

SIX

Step 6   Taking Notes

As you review the sources you have found, begin the process of taking notes on what you are finding out about the topic.

Here is a handy method for taking notes and getting ready to write your paper. Label each source that you have found (books, articles, pamphlets, encyclopedia entries, articles off the internet and so on) with a number (1,2,3,4,5) so that you can keep track of each source. These numbers are strictly for your tracking purposes.

Start reading your materials and underline or highlight points of interest. As you make these notes either on a legal pad or on the articles themselves, always remember to write the number you assigned by the note as well as the page number if there is one.

After taking notes, cut out significant quotes making sure to mark each quote with your reference number and page number. Cut out parts of the articles you copied and place your reference number on each. Cut out the notes from your legal pad as well. Each strip of paper will have the reference number and page number, so you will be able to shuffle them however way you wish.

Next, separate the strips of paper according to the major headings or categories of your research paper. Because you have decided beforehand what your headings will be, it should be easy to see into which category each quote or paraphrase fits.

As you sort through all your notes, you will see a pattern emerge, and your research will start to take a certain direction and form.

Remember that you are not necessarily reading every word of these documents. You are skimming your materials to find something of interest, something vital to your research. When something catches your eye, then you can stop and read in a more in-depth manner.

If you are reviewing a book, you do not have to read the entire book to use information from it. Look at the back of the book at the index to find the subject matter that pertains to your topic, then read that section of the book. With articles, you want to zero in on those sections of articles that coincide with your areas of interest. After you have taken notes on all of your sources and cut them out, set them aside for inclusion in your paper.

Now you have compiled a wealth of information on your topic in a manageable, clearly identified format. These strips of paper, which are like note cards, can be used within the text of your paper to present and develop your ideas and back up what you are writing.

Hint: The more notes you take the better, then you will have many from which to choose.

How *I* Did It...

The first thing I did to start the **note-taking** process was to get comfortable with a cup of tea, gather all my articles and books in a neat stack, and label each with a number, circling the number to distinguish it from other markings. Now each source had its own identifying number.

As I perused each article, I wrote at the top of the article the name of the heading to which it pertained. For instance, if it referred to "treatment," I marked it accordingly, "treatment," and so on. As I skimmed the articles, I underlined important thoughts and highlighted others. I never highlight whole blocks of information, just key words, then the important information is more distinct for me.

Some articles I tossed; they just were not interesting enough or relevant to my topic. Others I could see would be crucial in my understanding and development of the paper. I had gathered together about 30 articles and books, so this process took several weeks.

At first, I went completely through and read every article. After I went through the stack, I went back for a more thorough review. I took notes in the margins sometimes asking myself questions that might be answered in yet another article. In other words, I really became familiar with these materials as they began to broaden my understanding of my topic.

I did not conduct an interview for my paper, but, in a way, the whole project was a perpetual interview with myself! My personal perspective became an important anchor for understanding stress-related illness. By the time I had completed this step, I was very familiar with the authors I had found and their thoughts on my topic.

SEVEN

Step 7 Outline

Use your headings from the mind map as a base for your outline. They will serve as the Roman numerals in the outline. Construct the outline from your notes, emphasizing your areas of interest. This will organize your research project. Include a lot of detail as to the levels you wish to explore.

The outline will be based on your brainstorming mind map and your notes from the review of your sources. With the information you have reviewed, you can construct an outline that will detail the direction of your research.

Study the outline I constructed on my research topic. You can see that it is very detailed. If your outline is thorough enough, your research paper will write itself. This is a very important part of the research process since the outline becomes your road map. The more in-depth analysis you make at the outline level, the more organized and complete your paper will be in the end.

After constructing your outline, gather your sources together and label sources according to which aspects of the outline they cover. Mark your sources with the Roman numerals and letters from your outline.

As you explore all of your sources, the outline numbering becomes the one common thread that runs throughout your review of source materials.

The outline is your backbone and guide, so take extra time to organize it well. If you have a well-constructed outline, your paper will really flow! It is important to categorize all of your notes into the same headings as your outline. An added benefit is this will help you keep your sources organized as well.

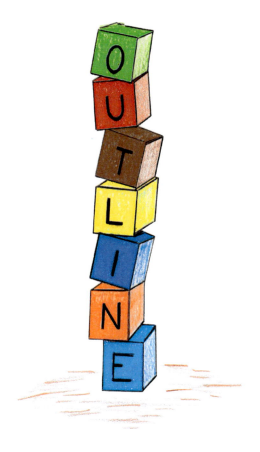

Hint: Your outline topics become your building blocks to success.

How *I* Did It...

Being a spontaneous spirit, I have always hated structure! I fought **outlines** for years, but once I got into the habit of creating an outline for my research papers, my life became so much easier. I finally got the connection between a detailed outline and an easy-to-write paper. When you have lots of information in your outline, your paper practically writes itself.

When you create an outline, your research really starts to come together in your head. Your ideas find a niche, and your direction becomes so much more distinct. In essence, you know where you're going. The road is familiar. You can still be very creative within the structure of an outline, but it serves as the road map for your research effort. It's important to remember that your outline is not set in stone. It can change as you go along. If you think of it as a living, changing organism, you are more likely to get into constructing it. Don't be afraid to alter your outline.

Because I had gone back and filled in my mind map with even more thoughts after reading some of the articles, I had a wealth of information to include in my outline. It suddenly became the culmination of all of my creative thoughts and the exposure to the many authors I had reviewed on my topic.

I used the major headings I had chosen as the Roman numerals of my outline. From there, I branched out into more specific areas to research. Under these subheadings, I included more detail. As you can see, my outline was fairly complete, and I'm so glad I spent a little time on it. It really paid off in the end and truly became my beacon in a fog of data. My outline gave me the final push to start actually writing my research paper!

EXAMPLE OF OUTLINE

What is the Best Approach to Controlling the Effects of Stress on the Human Body and Psyche?

I. **Overview**
- A. **Definition**
- B. **History**
- C. **Positive vs. Negative Stress**

II. **Origins of Stress**
- A. **External**
  1. **Environmental**
  2. **Noise Pollution**
  3. **Unhealthy Buildings**
- B. **Internal**
  1. **Loss of Locus of Control**
  2. **Low Self-Esteem**
  3. **History of Abuse (physical, verbal and psychological)**
  4. **Lack of Ability to Set Boundaries**
  5. **Suppressed Anger**

III. **Repercussions of Stress-Related Disease**
- A. **Physical**
  1. **Generalized Pain (head, neck, joints)**
  2. **Digestive Problems**
  3. **Respiratory (asthma)**
  4. **Circulatory (heart disease)**
  5. **Sleep Disorder**
  6. **Fatigue (Chronic Fatigue Syndrome)**
  7. **Sexual Dysfunction**
  8. **Nervous Disorders (Fybromyalgia)**
- B. **Psychological**
  1. **Anxiety (Panic Attacks)**
  2. **Memory Loss (Dementia)**
  3. **Depression**

C. Social
    1. Unemployment
    2. Poverty
    3. Dysfunctional Relationships
D. Spiritual
    1. Reduced Quality of Life
    2. Hopelessness
    3. Alienation from Self

IV. Physiology of Stress
A. Homeostasis – The Healthy Body
B. Etiology – The Nature of Disease
    1. Immune System
    2. Nervous System
    3. The Brain
    4. Emotions and the Adrenal Response
C. The Human Body under Stress

V. Treatments of Stress-Related Disease
A. External
    1. Pharmaceuticals (medications)
    2. Massage Therapy
    3. Acupuncture
    4. Yoga
    5. Vitamin/Mineral Supplements
    6. Diet/Nutrition
    7. Exercise
    8. Herbal Teas
B. Internal
    1. Meditation (Relaxation Response-RR)
    2. Psychotherapy (coping strategies)
    3. Diversion (hobbies)
    4. Stress Hardiness

VI. Findings
A. Hippocrates and the Natural Healing Force
B. Creating Positive Stress from Negative Stress
C. Holistic Approach
D. Integration of Mind, Body and Spirit

EIGHT

Step 8   Rough Draft

Your rough draft is your first attempt at writing your paper. Let the writing process flow. There is no need to be too concerned about form at this point. The important thing is to get something down on paper, and then the editing process will follow later.

Before starting your rough draft, read one of the sample research papers I wrote at the back of this booklet in order to get a feel for how your paper should be set up and also how your paper will be organized. Once you have reviewed my paper, decide if you are going to compose your paper at the computer or "cut and paste" it in your legal pad then enter it into the computer later.

Hint: Remember, you are driving the boat! Take charge of your research project.

On the computer, set up the first page of your paper (name, course, title, and date) according to MLA style, a title page and abstract according to APA style. Remember to insert your headings as well according to the appropriate style. At this point, while you are still fresh in the project, it is a good idea to go ahead and complete your Works Cited or References page (list of sources). You will really be glad that you took the time to do this in the beginning when your energy level is still very high as this is one of the most labor-intensive parts of your paper. Even if you do not use all the references in this original list, you can always go back when you are done and delete the ones you do not use. All authors and sources within your paper should be listed on the source page in alphabetical order by author. This is one of the first things your instructor will check.

Now you are ready to become an author. Always remember to use ONLY third person voice when writing a research paper, no first person pronouns (I, me, my) unless your professor instructs you to do so. You are writing in an objective way. You will end up expressing your opinion as a result of your research, but you will do so in the third person: "It can be concluded that..." or "It is apparent that...." The first person plural "we" is acceptable, however, when you are including your audience.

Start out with something really catchy. Your first sentence should get your reader hooked! Begin by writing in your own words about what you have read. In the first section, you will introduce your reader to your topic and lay out what you will be exploring. Your "voice" will be obvious in the paper. When you bring another "voice" or author (secondary source) into the discussion, you will need to document that source. In MLA style, you will include the name of the author (or abbreviated title if you have no author) and page number in parentheses after your quote each time you use information from one of your sources.

Notice that in MLA style direct quotes longer than three lines are indented five spaces in block paragraph form and are double-spaced. No quotation marks are required with these indented quotes because the indentation itself implies a quote. If you have a quote within the quote you are bringing into your paper, change the double quotation marks to single quotation marks as is always the case with a quote within a quote.

Lift the information out of the source document EXACTLY as you find it with direct quotes. If you mention the author or publication before the quote, you cite it with only the page number in parentheses. There is no need to mention the author's name again. Use the ellipsis to cut out parts of information and avoid very long quotes. Add brackets with your own words to make the part you piece together grammatically correct. In APA style, use the author and date of publication as well as the page number.

When putting information into your own words, remember that you have to significantly rephrase the words of the author to make it an indirect rather than a direct quote. You do not need to cite the author when paraphrasing until you are through, sometimes several paragraphs later. You can cite indirect quotes with a range of page numbers since you probably reviewed several pages for paraphrasing.

Finally, always remember that it is very important how you leave your reader. Just as the last scene in a movie lingers with us so will your final comments play in your reader's mind. As you finish up your rough draft, end your paper with a significant punch. The important thing is to let the reader know where your research has lead you. Leave the reader with something that will leave him/her thirsty for more. The thought-provoking way you leave your reader will make all your research worthwhile!

How *I* Did It...

I wrote my **rough draft** on a legal pad because I still like the feel of shuffling paper and producing a physical product. I'm never terribly careful when I start the rough draft of a research paper. After all, that's why they call it "rough." I knew that anything was subject to change. That's what writer's block is all about, trying to be perfect the first go-round. It is much better to just dive in and start writing. You can always change it later.

I laid out my outline, notes, articles and other resource materials and prepared to write. I put my sources in the same order as my outline in front of me along with my notes. I also made sure my articles had outline numbers on them which corresponded to the outline.

Using the outline, I started to write an introduction to my paper in my own words but in the third person. I used my articles to back up what I was saying. If I really liked an author, I cut out what he/she had said and cut and pasted it right into my paper using quotation marks. I made sure to cite my source with the author's name and page number in parentheses immediately after my quotation marks, making sure that the identifying number I had assigned that source was clearly marked.

Other times, I simply rephrased what an author had said in my own words. I did not cite this author until I was through using his/her information, sometimes several paragraphs later.

I was careful to follow my outline so that my paper would appear organized with a nice, logical sequence. Since I had spent a lot of time on the outline, the writing went fairly smoothly, and before I knew it, I had finished my first draft!

NINE

Step 9 Editing

After writing your rough draft, start a review of your research paper for grammar, content, organization and style—MLA, APA, Chicago Style of Writing, Turabian or whatever your professor has specified. The first edit will reveal the most obvious mistakes. Fine tuning will come later.

In the Information Age, we have many electronic devices at our disposal for correcting spelling and grammatical errors. If you have used Spell Check or Grammar Check along the way, your editing work will be simpler. Running your paper through these grammar devices is a good place to start your editing process. Be sure to use all your resources to produce the best possible copy for submission to your professor.

If grammar is your weakness, make sure to use these very valuable tools, and even if you are a grammar whiz, these tools will help you find typographical errors and spacing errors. If you are particularly insecure about your grammatical expertise, go to a tutoring lab at your school for help. This is completely acceptable and preferable. Your instructor will be impressed that you cared enough to work on your writing skills!

Next, look beyond grammar mechanics to organization:

- Have you included all the information you wanted to cover that is listed on the outline?
- Are the headings in the right order?
- Are your paragraphs well-organized with only relevant

- Does one paragraph logically lead to the next with a smooth transition?
- Have you used effective transitional phrases to make your paper flow (on the other hand, in other words, consequently, for the most part, overall, and so on)?

Review your work for content and style:

- Are all outside sources documented according to the style your instructor has required?
- Are all sources listed on your References or Works Cited page included in your paper and vice versa?
- Is all information relevant?
- Have you repeated yourself?
- Are your sources academic and scholarly?
- Have you closely followed the research style required by your professor?

Look at the sample research papers in this booklet to use as a guide. Notice the difference in quoting directly and indirectly. The author's name and page number appear immediately after the direct quote. When paraphrasing or indirect quoting, however, you cite the source several paragraphs later after you are through using that source.

Have you followed your outline? If you have, your paper will appear organized and easy-to-follow. Make sure you have discussed your topic in a timely, understandable sequence. If you are unsure about certain facts or observations, now is the time to do a little further research to substantiate your findings.

If you have not done so, consider adding pertinent documents as appendices. An appendix is included after your Works Cited or References page. It is not included in the pagination of your paper.

As an example, you could include your interview as an appendix in its entirety if you think it would be of interest to the reader. If you have written a particularly technical paper with many unusual terms, you might want to consider adding a glossary defining terms that you have used as an appendix. A map, survey, questionnaire, charts or graphs are also appropriate appendices. Remember to name each one, Appendix A, Appendix B and so on.

Read your rough draft over several times. It is a good idea to let it sit a day or two and come back to it. When we view our work with fresh eyes the next day, we often see things we have overlooked. Call this "steep" time as though you were brewing a nice cup of tea!

When you come back to your rough draft after letting it sit for a day or two, you'll be surprised at the glaring mistakes you might have overlooked before giving it a rest. Research can be a pretty intense process, and sometimes we just have to set it aside for awhile. Take a break! Take a nap! Catch a movie! It will still be there when you return.

> Hint: Let your paper sit a day before you edit in order to read it with "new" eyes.

Finally, the most important aspect of doing research is the reader must know where you have presented original thoughts and where you have gone to other sources to find information. Copyrights protect an author's work as his/her sole domain. You would not want someone to steal your work, so always remember to give credit where credit is due.

Plagiarism or scholastic dishonesty implies you have copied someone else's work without properly documenting it. In the age of abundant information, a student might be tempted to purchase work off the internet and plagiarize it as his/her own. This is a very serious offense. It will not only net you an "F" for the course but could get you removed from your institution; therefore, your degree and academic future would be in jeopardy.

Remember, it works both ways: your professors can find ready-made term papers just as easily as you!

Hint: Stealing someone else's work or purchasing and presenting work as your own is plagiarism and is a dangerous legal and moral issue.

How *I* Did It...

Editing the sample research paper in this booklet was one of the most difficult tasks I have ever taken on, mainly because I knew it would be scrutinized by the public, my students and my colleagues. Maybe you should all imagine your work being published, and perhaps then you would be more careful about editing! I always, however, came back to the concept that I was "driving the boat." Whatever the public or my students or my colleagues thought really wasn't as important as my own standard of excellence that I had set. When writing a paper, a book, anything, you have to please yourself first. Be true to yourself, and you will always be proud of your work.

Even though I am an English professor and presume I know a little more than average about English usage and style, I still used a lot of resources to edit my paper. There are limitations to Spell Check (many words are not in the database) and Grammar Check (some suggestions are simply stylistic), but yet they are still our best bet for editing grammar, especially the first time around.

As far as editing for MLA style, I went to the MLA website and reviewed sample papers. I always tried to find an example at least somewhat like the one I was working on, whether it was a reference citing or a layout. I made sure that what was listed on the Works Cited page was, in fact, cited within the text of my paper. In addition, I made sure that any author I had cited in my research paper was listed on the Works Cited page. I did likewise for the APA paper. I made sure I had done my best in writing the best possible papers for my students.

TEN

Step 10 Final Copy

Before submitting your paper, make sure it is your very best effort. Check for grammatical mistakes and MLA or APA stylistic errors one more time.

This step involves very carefully going over your paper with a fine-toothed comb. You want to look at every word and make sure you have put forth your very best effort. You cannot do this quickly. It is a good idea to read it, then put it down for a day or two and come back to it. What you did not see before might stand out as a glaring issue the next time you read it. You should read and re-read your paper four or five times before turning it in, making sure it is a quality paper. This means, of course, that if you procrastinate and wait until the very last minute (as we sometimes do!), you will not have ample time to go over it. Even if you are running late, you STILL need to read over your paper several times before submitting it to your professor.

Most importantly, you should take a great deal of pride in the fact that you have produced a quality paper. After having followed all the steps in this booklet, you have an excellent chance of just having written an outstanding research paper, one of which you can be very proud!

How *I* Did It...

Editing the **final copy** was a challenge. Writing is such a personal process. I've learned that in my years of teaching. Sometimes, I'll talk to a student who is really fearful about writing, and I will discover that it was some negative comment a high school English teacher made that stuck with the student. Don't let these thoughts hold you back. Maybe she was wrong about your writing abilities! I certainly had teachers who didn't think I would make it in this field. We are ALL good writers with enough effort and polish.

Because of this very personal connection to our own writing style, the final edit in a writing project is the hardest step. It is so difficult to look at our own writing objectively, but remember, this last step is truly the light before the dawn! Our egos become attached to a writing assignment. We are so sensitive about what people say about our writing. I know I really am since that is my chosen field, but in the end, hard work pays off!

At any rate, I had to take off my ego and be willing to look at my writing in a very objective way with the final edit. I had to ask myself how others would view it. Would students relate to it? More importantly, would they learn from it? It really helped me to let the paper sit for awhile in between edits. I say 'in between' because I looked at it a NUMBER of times!

Now that it is done, I see that there are ten steps to this research process, but really they all lead to one ultimate end: the final edit. It is the most important step and the most difficult but by far the most rewarding. Hopefully, you, dear students, will feel the same pride after completing your quality research paper that I did and write many, many more great research papers!

MLA Format Guidelines

1. Use one-inch margins all the way around and use 12-pt font. Choose a font style that is readable—avoid script. Double space entire document.

2. On the top of the first page and flush with the left margin, put your name, instructor's name, course name, and date. Notice that the date is in European style with no commas (17 March 2011). All of this information is double-spaced. There is no title page in MLA format.

3. Center the title of your paper under this information using title case (capitalizing important words).

4. Double space between the title and the first line of the text. Do not underline title or put it in quotation marks.

5. Use italics for long works (books, journals, or newspapers) and quotation marks for shorter works (articles, essays, or names of chapters). Italicize all foreign words.

7. Set up a one-half inch header to the far right with your last name and page number on every page.

8. List references and sources on a Works Cited page. This page should have the same header as the rest of the paper.

9. Block indent one-half inch and double space direct quotes longer than three lines. Quotation marks are not used in an indented quote as the indentation itself implies a quote. Use single quotation marks for a quote within a quote.

10. All sources are listed by author in alphabetical order on the Works Cited page. If an author is not given, use the title. Personal interviews are cited by last name of the interviewee and date interviewed.

12. Include the author's last name and page number in parentheses immediately after direct quotes within your paper. When paraphrasing (putting information into your own words), list the author and page number in parentheses after you are through using that source. This is usually several paragraphs later. Use a shortened title when author is not given.

13. The *MLA Handbook for Writers of Research Papers* comes out in new editions every few years. You can find the most current edition at the MLA site listed below. *The Owl At Purdue—Free Writing Help and Teaching Resources,* published at Purdue University, is also a great source for MLA documentation.

14. Some of the changes with the new 7th edition include italicizing instead of underlining; no longer listing URLs; and identifying media type such as print, web, video, DVD, TV and so on. New abbreviations include N.p. (no publisher), n. pag. (no pagination), and n.d. (no date).

15. Section headings in MLA style have specific formats. Level 1 is bold, flush left; Level 2 is in italics, flush left; Level 3 is centered and bold; Level 4 is centered and in italics and Level 5 is underlined and flush left. The first paragraph after the heading is not indented.

Source: *MLA Handbook for Writers of Research Papers,* 7th ed., by the Modern Language Association (Author), 2009.

Academic Websites

www.mla.org—MLA Style
www.apa.org—APA Style
www.chicagomanualofstyle.org
http://owl.english.purdue.edu

Research Styles

I have included two sample research papers in this booklet for you to follow. One is written in MLA style and the other is written in APA style. These are the most common research styles required by teachers although there are several others including Chicago Style of Writing, Campbell's, Turabian and others. Sometimes professors will identify a specific style for you to use, and in other instances, no specific format is required. A professor may give you a handout which explains only their particular requirements. Of course, you should respect the specific guidelines of your instructor. After all, your professor is the one with the power to give you an "A." If no particular style is required, it is still a good idea to use one of the formatted styles, just to keep yourself on track.

The following sample research papers will be a valuable guide for you to follow when writing your research paper. Sit down and read them thoroughly, whether MLA or APA, before you start writing your paper. As you read, notice how the paper is set up. where my thoughts or interpretations are obvious and where I have included the views of other writers. Study how the categories fall into place. One logically leads to the other. The thesis statement is in bold on the first page. Finally, make note of all the MLA or APA stylistic features. There are specific characteristics associated with each style. After thoroughly reading the sample paper, you are ready to start your own research effort!

Sample MLA Paper

Rockman 1

Jane Rockman

Professor Georgantonis Keah

English 1301

29 June 2012

What is the Best Approach to Controlling

the Effects of Stress on the Human Body and Psyche?

Overview

> "I have known a great many troubles,
>
> But most of them never happened."
>
> —Mark Twain (Kerr)

Twain said it well. Many times stress is nothing more than a

perceived threat, but whether that threat is real or not, the

body responds in the same way: increased heart rate, faster

breathing and a rush of blood to muscle tissue in the skin,

hands and feet. The wear and tear on the body can be enor-

mous. Stress in humans involves how an individual interacts

with the environment when his/her well-being is threatened.

The perceived threat is different for each person, but the

physiological results are the same. How we react to stress

becomes a learned pattern, and unless specific steps are tak-

en to break the pattern, it remains the same throughout our

lifetimes. **One thing is clear: the effects of stress on the**

Rockman 2

human body and psyche are totally within our control as thinking individuals.

Response to environmental threats has been part of the human make-up ever since the birth of human-kind. Theorists have always suspected that because man evolved with a sophisticated brain, the thought process itself of whether to fight or give flight impacts the health of the human body and mind:

> In 1941, physiologist Walter B. Cannon, Harvard Medical School, defined what he later termed the fight-or-flight response. When the brain perceives stress, it signals the sympathetic branch of the autonomic nervous system, which regulates the 'automatic' functions of the body, such as the heartbeat and the digestive processes (Garfield 136).

The history of etiology, or the study of disease, has always led scientists to examine the mind-body relationship, but in the eyes of Louis Pasteur as expressed in his germ theory, it is the strength of the invading microbe and not the health of the organism's immune system that dictates the outcome of a patient's illness.

Rockman 3

With the financial support of John D. Rockefeller, Pasteur led the medical community into the world of immunizations, antibiotics and the pharmaceutical industry it exists today (Seaward, *Managing Stress...*50). Traditional medical treatment today evolved from these first attempts of Pasteur to explain illness. His greatest challenger was Claude Bernard, a French physiologist, who first used the term "homeostasis," which is defined as "the tendency of an organism or a cell to maintain internal equilibrium by adjusting its physiological processes" (*American Heritage* 650). Bernard maintained that it was not the germs that caused disease but the unhealthy condition of the body when the germ invades:

> Bernard suggested that good living practices, including one's attitude and sound nutrition, were essential to keep the body at its optimal level of health, thereby creating an infertile and inhospitable place for the seeds of microorganisms to germinate (Seaward, *Managing Stress...*50).

Bernard used the analogy of the seed (invading microbe) and the soil (the body) to demonstrate this theory, and he was met with much opposition from the traditional medical community, including Pasteur; however, even on his

Rockman 4

deathbed, admitted what Bernard always believed to be true: "Bernard is right, [it's not the seed], it's the oil" (Seaward, *Managing Stress*...50). Pasteur concurred with Bernard: the healthy body repels disease.

More recently, scientists are starting to see a clear bi-directional link between the immune and the nervous systems. It appears that these two systems interact to either promote disease or enhance the chances for a healthy body. Robert Ader, who first used the term "psychoneuroimmunology," defines it as "the emerging field that studies an organism's response to experience and the bodily system that operates to defend an organism against disease" (Garfield 136). More than ever, it is believed that "mind over matter" is more than just an expression. Physical health is greatly influenced by the patient's state of mind: the healthier the mind, the healthier the body.

Hans Selye, Director of the Institute of Experimental Medicine and Surgery, Montreal, first used the phrase "stress syndrome" in 1936. He clearly identified stress-induced body responses as biological, measurable phenomena verified through scientific techniques. Until that point, stress was a vague concept tied to the rising cost of living or the fast pace

Rockman 5

of society. He differentiated, however, between *distress* (negative stress) and *eustress* (positive stress). He observed that the body goes through the same nonspecific responses whether the stimulus is positive or negative. He maintained that "stress is not necessarily undesirable...[and that]...it all depends on how you take it. The stress of failure, humiliation, or infection is detrimental; but that of exhilarating creative successful work is beneficial" (Selye). It was his belief that, unlike the lower animals, humans are compelled to fight for goals of accomplishment or what might be called "eustress." This driving need to achieve perpetuates evolution on an emotional and a spiritual level.

Origins of Stress

In the world today, there are many sources of distress or negative stress. Seaward (*Stand Like Mountain...*7) asserts that negative stress is a form of imbalance: "Flat tires, delayed flights, bounced checks, phone tag, long checkout lines, flippant adolescents, cancerous tumors and backed-up traffic can all disturb our psychic equilibrium." He goes on to identify characteristics of negative stress such as impatience, anger, frustration, feelings of helplessness and anxiety, even boredom, as contributors to a negative stress response. Strong

Rockman 6

emotions are a necessary catalyst to accomplish our goals but only when they are channeled into positive thoughts and actions. Positive stress is high energy productive activity within a setting of emotional balance. Disease takes over when emotional challenges are left unresolved and un-channeled: "In the worst-case scenario, the body becomes the battlefield for the war games of the mind" (Seaward, *Stand Like Mountain...*7). In a world of cell phones, noise pollution, environmental catastrophes and unhealthy build-ings, there is fertile ground for stress-related diseases. It has even been postulated that one of the greatest sources of modern-day stress is man's alienation from Nature (Wein 2). In a sea of societal issues, both physical and mental, it is a highly individual matter how each of us responds to dis-tress signals. Couple these external forces with the every-day drama of our lives, and it is not difficult to accept that, "An estimated 75 to 85 percent of all health-related prob-lems are caused or aggravated by stress" (Kerr).

Why are some individuals more prone to these ill-nesses than others? An important aspect of dealing with stress is one's sense of the origins of events or one's "locus

Rockman 7

of control." Feelings of powerlessness demonstrate this loss of locus of control and are a significant factor in stress-related illness. Other factors include low self-esteem; history of physical, verbal and psychological abuse; inability to be assertive and set boundaries; suppressed anger and self-alienation. These internal factors are the variables which determine how we respond to stress and its potential to wreak havoc on the body.

Repercussions of Stress-Related Disease

Stress—left undirected into positive outlets—takes its toll on the human body and psyche affecting all aspects of life. Adverse physical effects include generalized pain throughout the body, digestive problems, respiratory illness, heart disease, sleep disorders, fatigue, hair loss, blurry vision, sexual dysfunction and nervous disorders.

The psychological effects are just as profound. Stress-related mental characteristics and disorders include panic attacks, memory loss, depression, agoraphobia, disorientation, anxiety and other emotional illnesses.

From a social perspective, left unchecked, negative stress can have a devastating effect on one's life. Possible

Rockman 8

social implications include unemployment, poverty, dysfunctional relationships, loss of mobility, underachievement, dependence and inability to cope with or adjust to societal changes. Finally, the effects on the human psyche, one's sense of spirituality, are the most devastating repercussions of all: restlessness (angst), feelings of not being fulfilled, hopelessness and alienation from self, all resulting in a greatly reduced quality of life.

Physiology of Stress

Cannon, in his book, *The Wisdom of the Body*, first came up with the term "homeostasis" in 1939:

> The coordinated physiological processes which
> maintain most of the steady states in the organism
> are so complex and so peculiar to living beings—
> involving as they may, the brain and nerves, the
> heart, lungs, kidneys and spleen, all working
> cooperatively—that I have suggested a special
> designation for these states, *homeostasis*. It
> means a condition which may vary, but which is
> relatively constant (Cziko 56).

Rockman 9

The human body, along with other mammals, has the ability
to adjust to variables in the external environment by main-
taining the internal physiological systems of the body. Examples of this control can be seen in body temperature, blood
pressure and acid-base balance ("Definition of Homeostasis"). This ability is achieved through a system of control
mechanisms, which are alerted through negative feedback,
for example: "a high level of carbon dioxide in extracellular
fluid triggers increased pulmonary ventilation, which in turn
causes a decrease in carbon dioxide concentration" ("Homeostasis"). The lungs can and will automatically respond to a
distress signal.

     Selye explored the mechanisms of stress-induced
bodily responses. He discovered that

> ...stress itself is not a nonspecific reaction. The
> pattern of the stress reaction is very specific:
> it affects certain organs (e.g., the adrenal, the thy-
> mus and the gastrointestinal tract) in a highly selec-
> tive manner. When dealing with an impending
> challenge, such as a deadline, the stress-response
> is helpful in slowing down certain bodily processes

Rockman 10

like digestion, growth and reproduction so that

the stressor can be addressed (3-4).

The etiology of stress-generated diseases is closely

tied to the immune system. When it is working properly, the

immune system maintains homeostasis in the body; howev-

er , in conditions of overreaction or under-reaction, the im-

mune system breaks down causing infection or disease

(Seaward, *Managing Stress...* 54). From Selye's work and

Seward's follow-up, it can be concluded that stress wreaks

havoc on the body at a cellular level in a very particular way.

In other words, stress-related diseases are not psychosomatic

in nature but very real.

Dr. Esther Sternberg, Director of the Integrative

Neural Immune program at NIH's (National Institutes of

Health) National Institute of Mental Health (NIMH), has

made great strides in understanding how immune molecules

work. She discovered that the part of the brain that controls

the stress response is continually activating stress hormones,

which basically tell the immune cells to not fight a bacteria

or a virus. In cases of chronic stress, the immune cells are

less likely to respond to danger signals of the body (Wein 2).

Rockman 11

The hypothalamus is the part of the brain that controls the stress response. Through hormones released by the pituitary and adrenal glands, it causes the cortisol level in the body to rise. Cortisol is the steroid hormone that assists us in stressful encounters. Unfortunately, the brain also uses cortisol to suppress the immune system. Stress acts upon the median eminence (ME) of the hypothalamus. Nervous stimuli come from the cerebral cortex of the brain and reach neuroendocrine cells located in the ME. It is important to note that the hypothalamus is that part of the brain dealing with emotions. The limbic system is a group of nerve pathways controlling mood and emotion. It is also linked with the autonomic nervous system and some stress-related illnesses, such as anxiety and depression, which are a result of hormonal and autonomic changes ("Know Your Brain"). The implication of these physiological phenomena is that the immune system is greatly influenced by emotional stress (Seaward, *Managing Stress* 54).

It was Candace Pert, former Chief of Brain Chemistry at the National Institute for Mental Health, who made the discovery that immune cells have built-in receptor sites for

Rockman 12

neuropeptides, which are neurotransmitters produced by the

brain with a similar effect as opiates. These cells impact

everything from mood swings to immune system function.

Pert discovered that these neuropeptides are not solely pro-

duced by the brain; she found that not only do neuropeptides

have receptors in the immune cells but also the immune cells

themselves can produce them. Further, immune cells appear

to have a memory of emotional responses. Neuropeptides are

the communication link between the brain and T– and B-

cells; that is, the immune system speaks to the brain and vice

versa. Pert concludes, therefore, that "emotions may sup-

press the function of lymphocytes while others may act as

immune-enhancers" (Seaward, *Managing Stress*...53). All of

this research has far-reaching implications for our under-

standing of stress-related disease:

> What all these studies seem to indicate is that there
>
> is a strong relationship between emotional
>
> responses and the biochemical changes they pro-
>
> duce...Whereas before Pert's findings it was
>
> believed cortisol played the crucial role in
>
> immune-suppression, it is now thought that

Rockman 13

structural changes in neuropeptides, influenced

by emotional thought, play the most significant

role in immuno-incompetence (Seaward,

Managing Stress 54).

Treatment of Stress-Related Disease

Treatment of stress-related disease involves two distinct

approaches: treating the external symptoms of the illness

and analyzing the internal manifestations of stress. The tra-

ditional approach to dealing with these illnesses involves

prescribing medications to treat pain or other drugs, which

alter the brain chemistry. More recently, however, nontradi-

tional approaches to the external symptoms include massage

therapy; hot mineral baths; acupuncture; yoga; vitamin and

mineral regimen; diet/nutrition analysis; physical exercise

activities; herbal tea consumption and creative outlets such

as dancing and listening to classical music as well as main-

taining a healthy sex life. Understanding the internal mani-

festations of stress from the inside out is crucial to surviving

in a world full of stressors.

It is possible to change a person's response to

stress. The term "stress hardiness" is a person's capacity to

Rockman 14

stay healthy in stressful situations. A group of personality

traits that stress-hardy people have include the following:

"believing in the importance of what they are doing; believ-

ing that they have some power to influence their situation;

and viewing life's changes as positive opportunities rather

than as threats" (Frey). Oftentimes, people afflicted with a

stress-related disease have lost their internal locus of control

or being in charge of their own destiny. They seem to have

a lowered self-esteem and a feeling of not being in control

of the events that surround them. They lack the assertive-

ness to clearly define a path and take it. They set up goals

but have trouble consummating them.

Psychotherapy often helps a person see how exteri-

or circumstances influence their decisions, resulting in a

feeling of helplessness and dependence. Any way a person

can regain a sense of self-worth and personal power is a

step in the right direction as far as treating stress-related

illness. Diversion is a good method of channeling negative

stress into positive results. Hobbies, reading, creative writ-

ing or any activity, which fosters individualism and confi-

dence will help the person with stress symptoms. The cycle

Rockman 15

can be broken. Research confirms that a positive attitude
can be crucial in dealing with a stress-related illness:

> Indeed, some studies show that personality traits
> like optimism and pessimism can affect many areas
> of your health and well-being. The positive think-
> ing that typically comes with optimism is a key
> part of effective stress management ("Stress Man-
> agement").

Finally, studies have clearly revealed that relaxation techniques such as meditation can be used to defeat
immunological diseases due to the fact that Relaxation Response techniques "counteract the stress response and decrease sympathetic nervous system responsivity, thereby
opposing stress-related deleterious immunological processes" (Esch, Fricchione and Stefano 24).

Relaxation Response, as found in transcendental
meditation, tai chi and other avenues, has been described by
Herbert Benson as the "physiological counterpart of the
stress of fight-or-flight response" (Esch et al. 25). During
RR, a person removes him/herself from an emotional reaction to his/her thoughts. Instead, focus is on a mantra
(monosyllabic word) allowing the mind a respite from the

Rockman 16

intensity of thought patterns. By not reacting emotionally to one's thoughts, great relaxation results. Within this relaxed state come several physiological changes in the body, which include "decreased oxygen consumption or carbon dioxide elimination (reduced metabolism), lowered heart rate, arterial blood pressure, and respiratory rate" (Esch et al. 24). It is not hard to see that meditation creates the diametrically opposite effect of negative stress on the human body. More and more research is being done to substantiate this remarkable solution to the detrimental effects of stress on the human body. The process of meditation has the profound ability to return the body to homeostasis. The process of meditation—separating one's emotional reaction to thoughts from bodily functions—breaks down the detrimental effects of stress on the body.

Findings

Everyone has a doctor in him or her; we just have to help it in its work. The natural healing force within each one of us is the greatest force in getting well (Hippocrates). Hippocrates (460 BC—377 BC) who is the father of medicine and one of the many academicians from the Golden Age of Greece

Rockman 17

greatly respected the healing powers of the body. He takes
it one step further when he claims, "A person should consider that health is the greatest of human blessings, and learn
how by his own thought to derive benefit from his illnesses." Hippocrates believed in the power of thought over the
condition of the human body. If one can achieve homeostasis through meditation and deep relaxation of the body's
metabolic functions, then quality health is a matter of mind
over body.

It is not stressors that cause stress; it is the emotional reaction of each of us that turns stress into a positive
or a negative force. Stress is quite an individual phenomenon, and the first step in conquering a stress-related disease
is to identify those events which are acting as stressors in
one's life and do something about them. Grounding is
found in those life events that we find challenging and fulfilling whether that is writing a musical composition, planting a garden to watch it grow, or watching a football game.
It is up to the individual to find those activities, which will
result in eustress as opposed to distress.

A three-tiered approach from the physical, mental

Rockman 18

and spiritual perspectives must be adopted in dealing with a stress-related illness. From a physical viewpoint, yoga, a vitamin and mineral regimen, high water intake to replenish the body's fluids and a balanced and nutritional diet can all serve to fortify and heal the body. From a mental and psychological vantage point, the Relaxation Response, particularly through meditation, allows the body to return to homeostasis; thus, the meditation route addresses both the physical and the mental effects of stressors on the body and psyche (spirit). In addition, it appears that being in control of one's life decisions and direction can offer the vital empowerment needed to keep stressors at bay.

Finally, the holistic approach of integrating mind, body and spirit to lead the life one chooses to live is the best way to achieve the balance necessary for good health, physically, mentally and, most importantly, spiritually. It is clear that taking control of one's life is the shortest route to overcoming stress-related disease.

Rockman 19

Works Cited

Cziko, Gary. *The Things We Do: Using the Lessons of Bernard and Darwin to Understand the What, How, and Why of Our Behavior.* Cambridge: MIT P, 2000. Print.

"Definition of Homeostasis." *EverythingBio.* 2007. *Everything Bio.com.* Web. 16 Jan. 2007.

Esch, Tobias, Gregory L. Fricchione, and George B. Stefano. "The Therapeutic Use of the Relaxation Response in Stress-Related Diseases." *Medical Science Monitor* 9.2 (2003): RA23-34. Print.

Frey, Rebecca J. "Stress." *Health A-Z.* 1 July 2006. *Medical Network, Inc.* Web. 14 Aug. 2006.

Garfield, Eugene. "Psychoneuroimmunology: A New Facet of the Mind-Body Dialogue." *Current Comments.* 5 May 1986: 3-12. Web. 2 July 2006.

Hippocrates. "Quotations by Author." *The Quotations Page.* 2007. *Quotations Page.com.* Web. 17 January 2007.

"Homeostasis." *Biology-Online.* 2006. *Biology Online.org.* Web. 16 Jan. 2007.

"Homeostasis." *The American Heritage College Dictionary.* 3rd ed. 1993. Print.

Rockman 20

Kerr, Linda. "Stress Management." *Business People:* 25 May

2012. *businesspeople.com*. Web. 30 June 2012.

Seaward, Brian Luke. "Stress and Disease." *Managing*

Stress: Principles and Strategies for Health and Well-

Being. 5th ed. Boston: Jones and Bartlett, 2006. Web.

8 Jan. 2007.

---. *Stand Like Mountain Flow Like Water: Reflections on*

Stress and Human Spirituality. Deerfield Beach: Faith

Communications, 2006. Web. 8 Jan. 2007.

Selye, Hans. "The Nature of Stress." *International Center for*

Nutritional Research. 2010. International Center for

Nutritional Research, Inc. Web. 12 Jan. 2007.

"Stress Management—Positive Thinking: Reduce Stress

by Eliminating Negative Self-Talk." Mayo Clinic.

Mayoclinic.com. Web. 30 June 2012.

United States. National Institute of Neurological Disorders and

Stroke. *Brain Basics: Know Your Brain. NIH Publication*

No. 01-3440a. 8 Dec. 2005. Web. 4 Jan. 2007.

Wein, Harrison. "Stress and Disease: New Perspectives." *The NIH*

Word on Health. October 2000. United States. National

Institutes of Health. Web. 8 Jul. 2006.

APA Format Guidelines

1. Use one-inch margins all the way around and use 12-pt font. Choose a font style that is readable—avoid script. Double space entire document.

2. Include a title page, abstract and body. List sources on a separate References page. The title and 'Abstract' are not bolded, but the rest of the headings are bolded.

3. Unlike MLA style, APA style requires a title page. This includes the title of your paper, your name and your school. You can add an author's note at the bottom to include course name and instructor.

4. Set up a 'running head', a shortened title, which will appear on your title page and serve as your header. In the header, the running head will be flush left, in capital letters, and the page number will be flush right. This header will appear on every page, including the References page.

5. The abstract is included after the title page. It is a one-paragraph summation of the findings of the research, which is about 150-200 words, written in the past verb tense. This paragraph is not indented.

6. Double space between the title and the first line on the first page of your text. Do not underline the title or put it in quotation marks.

7. When directly quoting from a work, include the author's last name in a short phrase ("Smith found that...") in your paper, then cite the date of publication and page number in parentheses after the quote.

8. Use past verb tense when referring to research findings ('Smith concluded that...').

9. When using direct quotes longer than 40 words, block indent one-half inch and double space, omitting quotation marks. Use single quotation marks for a quote within a quote. Cite the date of publication and page number in parentheses after the blocked quote unless you have referred to the publication in your text then just cite the year of publication.

10. If you are paraphrasing, or putting the information into your own words from a source, you only need to identify the author and year of publication within your text, not in parentheses afterwards.

11. Personal interviews are not included on the References page. Cite the source within your paper—example:

    A. Smith, personal communication, July 12, 2012.

12. Use italics for long works (books, journals, or newspapers) and quotation marks for shorter works (articles, essays, or names of chapters).

13. List references and sources on a separate page called 'References.' All sources are listed by author in alphabetical order. The first line of an entry is flush left and subsequent lines are indented one-half inch in. Double spacing is used throughout. Note that in APA style, titles of sources are in sentence case (only the first word is capitaized), not title case as in MLA style.

14. All references that are cited in the text of your paper must also appear on the References page.

15. APA paper requirements vary. Use empirical method if your professor requires it; otherwise, use a standard introduction, body and conclusion with headings and References page.

16. An empirical APA paper includes a specific format. The first section is an introduction, which starts after the title on the first page of your text. This includes background information, a clearly-stated purpose of the research and importance, and then the hypotheses including a statement of why they are reasonable. A review of literature can also be included. The following headings follow: Method (with subheadings—Participants, Research Design, Measures and Procedure), Results, and Discussion. The References are on a separate page.

17. The *Publication Manual of the American Psychological Association* was updated in 2009 with the Sixth Edition. The most current edition is found at apa.org. *The Owl At Purdue—Free Writing Help and Teaching Resources,* published at Purdue University, is a reputable source for APA documentation.

18. APA section headings also have a specific format. Level 1 headings are centered, bold; Level 2 headings are flush left and bold; Level 3 headings are indented, bold and in sentence case (only first letter capitalized) with a period; Level 4 headings are indented, bold, italicized and in sentence case with a period and Level 5 headings are indented, italicized and in sentence case with a period. In Levels 3,4, and 5, start the body text after the period.

Source: *Publication Manual of the American Psychological Association,* Sixth Edition, by the American Psychological Association, July 2009.

Sample APA Paper

Running head: EFFECTS OF STRESS

What Is the Best Approach to Controlling the Effects of

Stress on the Human Body and Psyche?

Jane Rockman

Austin Community College

Author Note

This paper was prepared for English 1301 taught by

Professor Georgantonis Keah.

EFFECTS OF STRESS   2

Abstract

It is a well-known fact that stress factors are major contributors

to the deterioration of one's health. Review of the literature in

this area revealed that stress comes in two forms: negative stress

and positive stress. It was determined that there are internal

origins of stress, such as loss of locus of control, and external

sources of stress, such as environmental issues. It was also

discovered that the repercussions of a stress-related disease are

far-reaching and include physical manifestations, psychological

problems and social implications. Findings revealed that a holistic

approach integrating mind, body and spirit is most effective in

dealing with a stress-related illness, and gaining control over

one's life decisions can lead to this positive integration of mind,

body and spirit leading to the reduction of stress and

disease.

EFFECTS OF STRESS   3

What is the Best Approach to Controlling

the Effects of Stress on the Human Body and Psyche?

"I have known a great many troubles,

But most of them never happened."

—Mark Twain (Kerr, 2012)

Twain said it well. Many times stress is nothing more

than a perceived threat, but whether that threat is real or not,

the body responds in the same way: increased heart rate,

faster breathing and a rush of blood to muscle tissue in the

skin, hands and feet. The wear and tear on the body can be

enormous. Stress in humans involves how an individual

interacts with the environment when his/her well-being is

threatened. The perceived threat is different for each person,

but the physiological results are the same. How we react to

stress becomes a learned pattern, and unless specific steps

are taken to break the pattern, it remains the same throughout

our lifetimes. **One thing is clear: the effects of stress on**

the human body and psyche are totally within our control

as thinking individuals.

Response to environmental threats has been a part

of the human make-up ever since the birth of humankind.

Theorists have always suspected that because man evolved

EFFECTS OF STRESS   4

with a sophisticated brain, the thought process itself of

whether to fight or give flight impacts the health of the

human body and mind:

> In 1941, physiologist Walter B. Cannon, Harvard
>
> Medical School, defined what he later termed the
>
> fight-or-flight response. When the brain perceives
>
> stress, it signals the sympathetic branch of the
>
> autonomic nervous system, which regulates the
>
> 'automatic' functions of the body, such as the
>
> heartbeat and the digestive processes (Garfield,
>
> 1986, p. 136).

The history of etiology, or the study of disease, has

always led scientists to examine the mind-body relationship,

but in the eyes of Louis Pasteur as expressed in his germ

theory, it is the strength of the invading microbe and not the

health of the organism's immune system that dictates the

outcome of a patient's illness.

With the financial support of John D. Rockefeller,

Pasteur led the medical community into the world of

immunizations, antibiotics and the pharmaceutical industry

as it exists today (Seaward, 2006, p. 50). Traditional medi-

cal treatment today evolved from these first attempts of

EFFECTS OF STRESS   5

Pasteur to explain illness. His greatest challenger was

Claude Bernard, a French physiologist, who first used the

term "homeostasis," which is defined as "the tendency of an

organism or a cell to maintain internal equilibrium by ad-

justing its physiological processes" (*American Heritage,*

1993, p. 650). Bernard maintained that it was not the germs

that caused disease but the unhealthy condition of the body

when the germ invades:

> Bernard suggested that good living practices,
>
> including one's attitude and sound nutrition, were
>
> essential to keep the body at its optimal level of
>
> health, thereby creating an infertile and inhospita-
>
> ble place for the seeds of microorganisms to germi-
>
> nate (Seaward, 2006, p. 50).

Bernard used the analogy of the seed (invading

microbe) and the soil (the body) to demonstrate this theory,

and he was met with much opposition from the traditional

medical community, including Pasteur; however, even Pas-

teur, on his deathbed, admitted what Bernard always be-

lieved to be true: "Bernard is right, [it's not the seed], it's

the soil" (Seaward, 2006, p. 50). Pasteur concurred with

Bernard: the healthy body repels disease.

EFFECTS OF STRESS   6

More recently, scientists are starting to see a clear

bi-directional link between the immune and the nervous sys-

tems. It appears that these two systems interact to either

promote disease or enhance the chances for a healthy body.

Robert Ader, who first used the term "psychoneuro-

immunology," defines it as "the emerging field that studies

an organism's response to experience and the bodily system

that operates to defend an organism against disease" (Gar-

field , 1986, p. 136). More than ever, it is believed that

"mind over matter" is more than just an expression. Physi-

cal health is greatly influenced by the patient's state of mind:

the healthier the mind, the healthier the body.

Hans Selye (1936), Director of the Institute of Ex-

perimental Medicine and Surgery, Montreal, first used the

phrase "stress syndrome." He clearly identified stress-

induced body responses as biological, measurable phenome-

na verified through scientific techniques. Until that point,

stress was a vague concept tied to the rising cost of living or

the fast pace of society. He differentiated, however, be-

tween *distress* (negative stress) and *eustress* (positive stress).

EFFECTS OF STRESS   7

He observed that the body goes through the same nonspecif-

ic responses whether the stimulus is positive or negative. He

maintained that "stress is not necessarily undesirable…[and

that]…it all depends on how you take it. The stress of fail-

ure, humiliation, or infection is detrimental; but that of exhil-

arating creative successful work is beneficial" (Selye,

2010). It was his belief that, unlike the lower animals, hu-

mans are compelled to fight for goals of accomplishment or

what might be called "eustress." This driving need to

achieve perpetuates evolution on an emotional and a spiritu-

al level.

Origins of Stress

In the world today, there are many sources of dis-

tress or negative stress. Seaward (2006) asserted that nega-

tive stress is a form of imbalance: "Flat tires, delayed

flights, bounced checks, phone tag, long checkout lines, flip-

pant adolescents, cancerous tumors and backed-up traffic

can all disturb our psychic equilibrium." He goes on to

identify characteristics of negative stress such as impatience,

anger, frustration, feelings of helplessness and anxiety, even

boredom, as contributors to a negative stress response.

EFFECTS OF STRESS   8

Strong emotions are a necessary catalyst to accomplish our

goals but only when they are channeled into positive

thoughts and actions. Positive stress is high energy produc-

tive activity within a setting of emotional balance. Disease

takes over when emotional challenges are left unresolved and

un-channeled: "In the worst-case scenario, the body be-

comes the battlefield for the war games of the

mind" (Seaward, 2006). In a world of cell phones, noise

pollution, environmental catastrophes and unhealthy build-

ings, there is fertile ground for stress-related diseases. It has

even been postulated that one of the greatest sources of mod-

ern-day stress is man's alienation from Nature (Wein, 2007).

In a sea of societal issues, both physical and mental, it is a

highly individual matter how each of us responds to distress

signals. Couple these external forces with the everyday dra-

ma of our lives, and it is not difficult to accept that, "An esti-

mated 75 to 85 percent of all health-related problems are

caused or aggravated by stress" (Kerr, 2012).

  Why are some individuals more prone to these ill-

nesses than others? An important aspect of dealing with

stress is one's sense of the origins of events or one's "locus

EFFECTS OF STRESS   9

of control." Feelings of powerlessness demonstrate this loss

of locus of control and are a significant factor in stress-

related illness. Other factors include low self-esteem; history

of physical, verbal and psychological abuse; inability to be

assertive and set boundaries; suppressed anger and self-

alienation. These internal factors are the variables which

determine how we respond to stress and its potential to

wreak havoc on the body.

Repercussions of Stress-Related Disease

Stress—left undirected into positive outlets—takes

its toll on the human body and psyche affecting all aspects of

life. Adverse physical effects include generalized pain

throughout the body, digestive problems, respiratory illness,

heart disease, sleep disorders, fatigue, hair loss, blurry vi-

sion, sexual dysfunction and nervous disorders.

The psychological effects are just as profound.

Stress-related mental characteristics and disorders include

panic attacks, memory loss, depression, agoraphobia, disori-

entation, anxiety and other emotional illnesses.

From a social perspective, left unchecked, negative

stress can have a devastating effect on one's life. Possible

EFFECTS OF STRESS   10

social implications include unemployment, poverty, dys-

functional relationships, loss of mobility, underachievement,

dependence and inability to cope with or adjust to societal

changes.

Finally, the effects on the human psyche, one's

sense of spirituality, are the most devastating repercussions

of all: restlessness (angst), feelings of not being fulfilled,

hopelessness and alienation from self, all resulting in a

greatly reduced quality of life.

Physiology of Stress

Cannon (1932) in his book, *The Wisdom of the*

Body, first came up with the term "homeostasis":

> The coordinated physiological processes which
>
> maintain most of the steady states in the organism
>
> are so complex and so peculiar to living beings—
>
> involving as they may, the brain and nerves, the
>
> heart, lungs, kidneys and spleen, all working
>
> cooperatively—that I have suggested a special
>
> designation for these states, *homeostasis*. It
>
> means a condition which may vary, but which is
>
> relatively constant (Cziko, 2000, p. 56).

EFFECTS OF STRESS   11

The human body, along with other mammals, has the ability
to adjust to variables in the external environment by main-
taining the internal physiological systems of the body. Examples of this control can be seen in body temperature,
blood pressure and acid-base balance ("Definition of Homeostasis", 2007) through a system of control mechanisms,
which are alerted through negative feedback, for example: "a
high level of carbon dioxide in extracellular fluid triggers
increased pulmonary ventilation, which in turn causes a decrease in carbon dioxide concentration" (Homeostasis). The
lungs can and will automatically respond to a distress signal.

Selye explored the mechanisms of stress-induced
bodily responses. He discovered that

> ...stress itself is not a nonspecific reaction. The
> pattern of the stress reaction is very specific:
> it affects certain organs (e.g., the adrenal, the thy-
> mus and the gastrointestinal tract) in a highly selec-
> tive manner. When dealing with an impending
> challenge, such as a deadline, the stress-response
> is helpful in slowing down certain bodily processes

EFFECTS OF STRESS   12

like digestion, growth and reproduction so that
the stressor can be addressed.

The etiology of stress-generated diseases is closely
tied to the immune system. When it is working properly, the
immune system maintains homeostasis in the body; however, in conditions of overreaction or under-reaction, the immune system breaks down causing infection or disease
(Seaward, 2006, p. 54). From Selye's work and Seward's
follow-up, it can be concluded that stress wreaks havoc on
the body at a cellular level in a very particular way. In other
words, stress-related diseases are not psychosomatic in nature but very real.

Dr. Esther Sternberg, Director of the Integrative
Neural Immune program at NIH's (National Institutes of
Health) National Institute of Mental Health (NIMH), has
made great strides in understanding how immune molecules
work. She discovered that the part of the brain that controls
the stress response is continually activating stress hormones,
which basically tell the immune cells to not fight a bacteria
or a virus. In cases of chronic stress, the immune cells are
less likely to respond to danger signals of the body (Wein,
2000).

EFFECTS OF STRESS   13

The hypothalamus is the part of the brain that controls the stress response. Through hormones released by the pituitary and adrenal glands, it causes the cortisol level in the body to rise. Cortisol is the steroid hormone that assists us in stressful encounters. Unfortunately, the brain also uses cortisol to suppress the immune system. Stress acts upon the median eminence (ME) of the hypothalamus. Nervous stimuli come from the cerebral cortex of the brain and reach neuroendocrine cells located in the ME. It is important to note that the hypothalamus is that part of the brain dealing with emotions. The limbic system is a group of nerve pathways controlling mood and emotion. It is also linked with the autonomic nervous system and some stress-related illnesses, such as anxiety and depression, which are a result of hormonal and autonomic changes ("Know Your Brain", 2005). The implication of these physiological phenomena is that the immune system is greatly influenced by emotional stress (Seaward, 2006, p. 54).

It was Candace Pert, former Chief of Brain Chemistry at the National Institute for Mental Health, who made the discovery that immune cells have built-in receptor sites for

EFFECTS OF STRESS   14

neuropeptides, which are neurotransmitters produced by the

brain with a similar effect as opiates. These cells impact

everything from mood swings to immune system function.

Pert discovered that these neuropeptides are not solely pro-

duced by the brain; she found that not only do neuropeptides

have receptors in the immune cells but also the immune cells

themselves can produce them. Further, immune cells appear

to have a memory of emotional responses. Neuropeptides

are the communication link between the brain and T– and B-

cells; that is, the immune system speaks to the brain and vice

versa. Pert concludes, therefore, that "emotions may sup-

press the function of lymphocytes while others may act as

immune-enhancers" (Seaward, 2006, p. 53). All of this re-

search has far-reaching implications for our understanding of

stress-related disease:

> What all these studies seem to indicate is that there
>
> is a strong relationship between emotional
>
> responses and the biochemical changes they pro-
>
> duce…Whereas before Pert's findings it was
>
> believed cortisol played the crucial role in
>
> immune-suppression, it is now thought that

EFFECTS OF STRESS   15

structural changes in neuropeptides, influenced

by emotional thought, play the most significant

role in immuno-incompetence (Seaward, 2006,

p. 54).

Treatment of Stress-Related Disease

Treatment of stress-related disease involves two distinct

approaches: treating the external symptoms of the illness

and analyzing the internal manifestations of stress. The tradi-

tional approach to dealing with these illnesses involves pre-

scribing medications to treat pain or other drugs, which alter

the brain chemistry. More recently, however, nontraditional

approaches to the external symptoms include massage thera-

py; hot mineral baths; acupuncture; yoga; vitamin and min-

eral regimen; diet/nutrition analysis; physical exercise activi-

ties; herbal tea consumption and creative outlets such as

dancing and listening to classical music as well as maintain-

ing a healthy sex life. Understanding the internal manifesta-

tions of stress from the inside out is crucial to surviving in a

world full of stressors.

It is possible to change a person's response to

stress. The term "stress hardiness" is a person's capacity to

EFFECTS OF STRESS   16

stay healthy in stressful situations. A group of personality

traits that stress-hardy people have include the following:

"believing in the importance of what they are doing; believ-

ing that they have some power to influence their situation;

and viewing life's changes as positive opportunities rather

than as threats" (Frey, 2006). Oftentimes, people afflicted

with a stress-related disease have lost their internal locus of

control or being in charge of their own destiny. They seem

to have a lowered self-esteem and a feeling of not being in

control of the events that surround them. They lack the as-

sertiveness to clearly define a path and take it. They set up

goals but have trouble consummating them.

Psychotherapy often helps a person see how exteri-

or circumstances influence their decisions, resulting in a

feeling of helplessness and dependence. Any way a person

can regain a sense of self-worth and personal power is a step

in the right direction as far as treating stress-related illness.

Diversion is a good method of channeling negative stress

into positive results. Hobbies, reading, creative writing or

any activity, which fosters individualism and confidence will

help the person with stress symptoms. The cycle can be

EFFECTS OF STRESS   17

broken. Research confirms that a positive attitude can be
crucial in dealing with a stress-related illness:

> Indeed, some studies show that personality traits
> like optimism and pessimism can affect many areas
> of your health and well-being. The positive think-
> ing that typically comes with optimism is a key
> part of effective stress management (Mayo Clinic,
> 2011).

Finally, studies have clearly revealed that relaxation techniques such as meditation can be used to defeat
immunological diseases due to the fact that Relaxation Response techniques "counteract the stress response and decrease sympathetic nervous system responsivity, thereby
opposing stress-related deleterious immunological processes" (Esch, Fricchione & Stefano, 2003, p. 24).

Relaxation Response, as found in transcendental
meditation, tai chi and other avenues, has been described by
Herbert Benson as the "physiological counterpart of the
stress of fight-or-flight response" (Esch et al., 2003, p. 25).
During RR, a person removes him/herself from an emotional
reaction to his/her thoughts. Instead, focus is on a mantra

EFFECTS OF STRESS   18

(monosyllabic word) allowing the mind a respite from the

intensity of thought patterns. By not reacting emotionally to

one's thoughts, great relaxation results. Within this relaxed

state come several physiological changes in the body, which

include "decreased oxygen consumption or carbon dioxide

elimination (reduced metabolism), lowered heart rate, arteri-

al blood pressure, and respiratory rate" (Esch et al., 2003,

p. 24). It is not hard to see that meditation creates the dia-

metrically opposite effect of negative stress on the human

body. More and more research is being done to substantiate

this remarkable solution to the detrimental effects of stress

on the human body. The process of meditation has the pro-

found ability to return the body to homeostasis. The process

of meditation—separating one's emotional reaction to

thoughts from bodily functions—breaks down the detri-

mental effects of stress on the body.

Findings

Everyone has a doctor in him or her; we just have to help it

in its work. The natural healing force within each one of us

is the greatest force in getting well (Hippocrates). Hippocra-

tes (460 BC—377 BC) who is the father of medicine and one

of the many academicians from the Golden Age of Greece

EFFECTS OF STRESS   19

greatly respected the healing powers of the body. He takes it
one step further when he claims, "A person should consider
that health is the greatest of human blessings, and learn how
by his own thought to derive benefit from his illnesses."
Hippocrates believed in the power of thought over the condition of the human body. If one can achieve homeostasis
through meditation and deep relaxation of the body's metabolic functions, then quality health is a matter of mind over
body.

It is not stressors that cause stress; it is the emotional reaction of each of us that turns stress into a positive or a
negative force. Stress is quite an individual phenomenon,
and the first step in conquering a stress-related disease is to
identify those events which are acting as stressors in one's
life and do something about them. Grounding is found in
those life events that we find challenging and fulfilling
whether that is writing a musical composition, planting a
garden to watch it grow, or watching a football game. It is
up to the individual to find those activities which will result
in eustress as opposed to distress.

A three-tiered approach from the physical, mental

EFFECTS OF STRESS   20

and spiritual perspectives must be adopted in dealing with a stress-related illness. From a physical viewpoint, yoga, a vitamin and mineral regimen, high water intake to replenish the body's fluids and a balanced and nutritional diet can all serve to fortify and heal the body. From a mental and psychological vantage point, the Relaxation Response, particularly through meditation, allows the body to return to homeostasis; thus, the meditation route addresses both the physical and the mental effects of stressors on the body and psyche (spirit). In addition, it appears that being in control of one's life decisions and direction can offer the vital empowerment needed to keep stressors at bay.

Finally, the holistic approach of integrating mind, body and spirit to lead the life one chooses to live is the best way to achieve the balance necessary for good health, physically, mentally and, most importantly, spiritually. It is clear that taking control of one's life is the shortest route to overcoming stress-related disease.

EFFECTS OF STRESS

References

Cziko, G. (2000). *The things we do: Using the lessons of Bernard and Darwin to understand the what, how, and why of our behavior.* Cambridge, MA: MIT.

"Definition of homeostasis." (2007). *EverythingBio.com.* Retrieved from http://www.everythingbio.com/glos/definition.php?word=homeostasis

Esch, T., Fricchione, G. L. and Stefano, G. B. (2003).The therapeutic use of the relaxation response in stress-related diseases. *Medical Science Monitor,* 9.2: RA23-34.

Frey, Rebecca J. "Stress." *Health A-Z.* 1 July 2006. *Medical Network, Inc.* Retrieved from http://www.healthatoz.com/healthatoz/Atoz/stress.jsp

Garfield, E. (1986, May). Psychoneuroimmunology: A new facet of the mind-body dialogue. *Current Comments,* 3-12. Retrieved from http://www.garfield.library.upenn.edu/essays/v9p136y1986.pdf

Hippocrates. (2007, January). Quotations by author. *QuotationsPage.com.* Retrieved from http://www.quotationspage.com/quotes/Hippocrates/

"Homeostasis." (2006). *Biology-Online. Biology Online.org.* Retrieved from http://www.biology-online.org/dictionary/Homeostasis

Kerr, L. (2012, May). Stress management. *Business People.* Retrieved from http://www.businesspeople.com/Post/562/stress-management

EFFECTS OF STRESS   22

Mayo Clinic. (2011, May). Stress management—Positive thinking: Reduce

    stress by eliminating negative self-talk. *Mayo Foundation for Medi-*

    cal Education and Research. Retrieved from http://

    www.mayoclinic.com/health/positive-thinking/SR00009/

    NSECTIONGROUP=2

National Institute of Neurological Disorders and Stroke. (2010). *Brain*

    *basics: Know your brain. (*NIH Publication No. 01-3440a).

    Washington, DC: U.S. Government Printing Office. Retrieved from

    http://www.ninds.nih.gov/disorders/brain_basics/

    know_your_brain.htm

Seaward, B. L. (2006). *Stand like mountain flow like water: Reflections*

    on stress and human spirituality. Deerfield Beach: Faith Communi-

    cations.

Seaward, B. L. (2006). Stress and disease. *Managing stress: Principles and*

    strategies for health and well-being. 5th ed. Boston,MA: Jones and

    Bartlett. Retrieved from http://www.jblearning.com/

    samples/0763740411/TOC_and_Preface_Seaward_Managing_

    Stress_5e.pdf

Selye, H. (2010). The nature of stress. *International Center for Nutritional*

    Research. International Center for Nutritional Research, Inc. Re-

    trieved from http://www.icnr.com/articles/the-nature-of-stress.html

EFFECTS OF STRESS   23

The American heritage college dictionary 3rd ed. (1993). Boston: MA:

> Houghton Mifflin.

Wein, H. (2007, January). Stress affects both body and mind. *NIH News in*

> *Health.* United States. National Institutes of Health. Office of

> Communications and Public Liaison. Retrieved from http://

> newsinhealth.nih.gov/2007/January/docs/01features_01.htm

Research Topic Ideas

Health

What is the Etiology or Cause of Cancer in Today's Society?

What Is Homeostasis and How is it ~~Affected Through Meditation?~~

What are Theories into the Causes ~~of HIV and AIDS?~~

How does the Food and Drug Administration Influence the Health Care Industry?

How does Alternative Medicine Differ from Traditional Medicine?

What is the Effect of Diet and Nutrition on Overcoming Disease?

Why has the Incidence of Diabetes Drastically Increased in the U.S.?

What are the Causes and Treatments of Fibromyalgia?

Why is Obesity Becoming an American Epidemic?

Why has the Incidence of Autism Dramatically Increased in the U.S.?

Sociology

Can Watching Television Be Addictive?

How are Cell Phones Impacting Face-to-Face Communication?

What are the Physical Effects on the Brain of Cell Phone Use?

How Has the Use of Illicit Drugs Affected American Society?

What is the Influence of the Movie Industry over American Lifestyles?

Economics

Why Was the Federal Reserve Board Created in 1913 on Jekyll Island?

What is Fiat Money?

How Does the Bilderberg Group Influence Global Economics and Politics?

What is the History of the Exchange of Money?

Why Do Oil Prices Fluctuate Dramatically Impacting Global Economics?

Political Science

What is the History of the Term "New World Order"?

How has the 9/11 Tragedy Lead to the Loss of Human Rights in America?

What is the 9/11 Truth Movement?

How has Modern-Day Legislation Challenged the American *Constitution*?

What are the Patriot Acts and How Have They Limited American Freedoms?

How Extensive is American Military Involvement Worldwide and Why?

What is Bohemian Grove?

What is the Power of the Media over Prevailing Political Views?

What is the Illuminati?

Why Is the Skull and Bones Society a Secret Organization?

What is the North American Union?

Psychology

Why is the Psychopathic Personality Prevalent in Present-Day American Society?

What is the Phenomenon of Group-Think or Herd Instinct?

What are the Social Repercussions of Bipolar Disorder?

Writing a Research Paper

Science and Technology

How could Radio Frequency Identification Devices (RFIDs) As Imbedded Microchips Affect the Privacy of the Individual?

How Is Nanotechnology Being Used in the Medical Field?

What is HAARP (weather manipulation research)?

How Did Area 51 Come to Exist and Why?

What is Eugenics and How Is It Practiced Today ?

What are the Harms of Genetically-Modified Food?

Do Humans Impact Global Warming and Is It A Crisis?

What is the Evidence for the Existence of Extraterrestrial Beings?

How Did Hitler Use the American Eugenics Model of Indian Reservations to Carry out his Genocide Plans in Germany?

What are the Ethical Considerations of Cloning in Today's Society?

What are Chem-Trails and are They Harmful to Our Health?

Why Do Humans Use Less Than 15% of the Brain?

Physics

Quantum Physics: How Do We Create and Control Our Physical Realities?

Spirituality

What is the Evidence for the Existence of God?

What is the Philosophy of Jesus Christ of Nazareth and Was He the Son of God?

What is the Islamic Faith and Who is Mohammad?

Astrology

What is the Effect of Planet Positions in the Field of Astrology?

What Is the Impact of the Houses of the Zodiac on Our Everyday Lives?

What Happens in the Retrograde of Planets?

Anthropology

What is the History of *Homo Sapiens* as an Evolutionary Phenomenon?

Did Man Create the Weapon or Did the Weapon Create Man?

What are the Potential Effects of Cloning on *Homo Sapiens?*

History

How Did the Golden Age of Greece Influence Present-Day Society?

Which Ancient Civilizations Have Most Influenced Modern Times?

Language

What are the Foreign Influences on the English Language?

How has American English Language Usage Changed in Recent Times?